BREAKOUT BIOGRAPHIES

# EMMA WATSON

## Actress, Women's Rights Activist, and Goodwill Ambassador

**Tanya Dellaccio**

PowerKiDS press

New York

Published in 2018 by The Rosen Publishing Group, Inc.
29 East 21st Street, New York, NY 10010

First Edition

Editor: Elizabeth Krajnik
Book Design: Tanya Dellaccio

Photo Credits: Cover Michael Stewart/WireImage/Getty Images; p. 5 Rob Kim/Getty Images Entertainment/Getty Images; pp. 7 (top), 15 Stephen Lovekin/Getty Images Entertainment/Getty Images; pp. 7 (bottom), 9 (top), 11 (bottom) 7831/Gamma-Rapho/Getty Images; p. 9 (bottom) Hulton Archive/Getty Images; p. 11 (top) Everett Collection/Shutterstock.com; p. 13 Steven Senne/AP Images; p. 17 (top) TONY KARUMBA/AFP/Getty Images; p. 17 (bottom) Bloomberg/Getty Images; pp. 19 (top), 23 (bottom) Astrid Stawiarz/Getty Images Entertainment/Getty Images; p. 19 (bottom) TIMOTHY A. CLARY/AFP/Getty Images; p. 21 (top) Eduardo Munoz Alvarez/Getty Images Entertainment/Getty Images; p. 21 (bottom) KENA BETANCUR/AFP/Getty Images; p. 23 (top) Paul Morigi/WireImage/Getty Images; p. 25 (top) Jesse Grant/Getty Images Entertainment/Getty Images; p. 25 (bottom) Rodin Eckenroth/Getty Images Entertainment/Getty Images; p. 27 Ovidiu Hrubaru/Shutterstock.com; p. 29 Kevork Djansezian/Getty Images Entertainment/Getty Images.

Cataloging-in-Publication Data

Names: Dellaccio, Tanya.
Title: Emma Watson: actress, women's rights activist, and goodwill ambassador / Tanya Dellaccio.
Description: New York : PowerKids Press, 2018. | Series: Breakout biographies | Includes index.
Identifiers: ISBN 9781538326176 (pbk.) | ISBN 9781538325476 (library bound) | ISBN 9781538326183 (6 pack)
Subjects: LCSH: Watson, Emma, 1990–Juvenile literature. | Actors–Great Britain–Biography–Juvenile literature.
Classification: LCC PN2598.W25 D39 2018 | DDC 791.4302'8092 B–dc23

Manufactured in the United States of America

CPSIA Compliance Information: Batch #BW18PK For Further Information contact Rosen Publishing, New York, New York at 1-800-237-9932

# CONTENTS

# MAKING A DIFFERENCE

For most actors, fame comes gradually. Only after many **auditions** and small parts in low-cost productions does their career begin to grow. This, however, was not the case for Emma Charlotte Duerre Watson. Watson's career began when she was very young, and it took little time for her to be recognized around the world.

Today, Watson uses her fame to encourage change. She uses her influence to fight for **gender** equality and to highlight issues concerning women's rights. Watson promotes the idea that through learning, understanding, and talking about important issues, the world can be a better place for everyone. From her role in the Harry Potter films to her work as an **activist**, Emma Watson has become a household name.

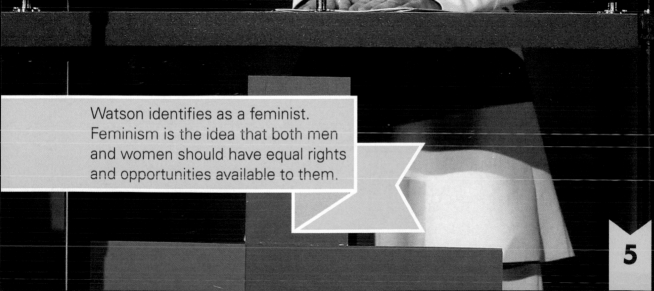

Watson identifies as a feminist. Feminism is the idea that both men and women should have equal rights and opportunities available to them.

5

# LANDING THE PART

Watson was born in Paris, France, on April 15, 1990. She moved to Oxfordshire, England, with her mother and brother after her parents divorced when she was five years old.

Both of her parents are lawyers, but Watson knew early on that she wanted to follow a different career path. She attended the Dragon School, a boarding and day school for boys and girls 4 to 13 years old in Oxford. Many successful men and women have attended this school. She was also a student at the Stagecoach Theatre Arts School. At Stagecoach, Watson took singing, acting, and dancing lessons.

When Watson was nine years old, she auditioned for her first professional acting role. After eight auditions, she landed the part of Hermione Granger in the film **adaptation** of *Harry Potter and the Sorcerer's Stone*.

# EMMA WATSON'S FAMILY

Watson is the oldest of Chris Watson and Jacqueline Luesby's two children. Watson's full brother, Alex, is three years younger than her. Watson has a half brother, Toby, and twin half sisters, Nina and Lucy. They share the same father, but have different mothers.

**ALEX WATSON**

Watson was studying at Stagecoach when she auditioned for the role of Hermione. Although she had taken part in school plays, this was her first professional acting job.

# YOU'RE A WIZARD, EMMA!

Watson signed on for one of the leading roles in the first of eight Harry Potter films based on the books written by J. K. Rowling. The books take place in a fictional world of witchcraft and **wizardry** and follow the lives of those who live in it. More specifically, they follow the lives of three friends: Hermione, Emma's character; Ron Weasley; and Harry Potter, the main character. The Harry Potter movies became one of the most popular and profitable film series in history.

The first film, *Harry Potter and the Sorcerer's Stone*, was released in November 2001 when Watson was 11 years old. She signed on for the remaining seven films and continued her education through homeschooling, much of which occurred on set.

**RUPERT GRINT**

**DANIEL RADCLIFFE**

Watson starred alongside Daniel Radcliffe (Harry Potter) and Rupert Grint (Ron Weasley). Both Radcliffe and Grint were 11 years old when they were cast for their roles in the films.

## ACCIO LINES!

Watson was very familiar with the Harry Potter books when she was cast as Hermione. During filming, she knew not only her lines, but everyone else's lines too. Sometimes she would accidently mouth the other characters' parts as they were acting. They would often need to reshoot the scenes when this happened. Watson says even though the silly quirk, or odd habit, is now a little embarrassing, she was very committed to doing the best job she could at such a young age.

# HERMIONE GRANGER

Since Watson loved reading the Harry Potter books, playing the role of Hermione was an opportunity for her to play one of her **heroines**. The character of Hermione is known for her intelligence and cleverness. She fought alongside Harry and Ron to defeat a dark force in the wizarding world—Lord Voldemort.

The character of Hermione is very involved in her education. The books and films focus on her love of reading and learning. Hermione's knowledge helps her friends succeed both in the classroom and in their adventures in the wizarding world. During their seven years in school, they face many challenges of character and skill. Watson and her costars grew up on the Harry Potter set. Acting the part of Hermione created many similarities between Watson and her character.

Watson says she and Hermione share a lot of the same qualities. Watson's personality went into Hermione, and Hermione shaped who Watson is today.

# A WIZARD AND A SCHOLAR

The amount of time and effort required to balance making the Harry Potter films with having a normal childhood was difficult for Watson at such a young age. She struggled with her decision to join the cast for the last two Harry Potter films. Watson wanted to focus on her education and felt it might not be possible while filming.

The team involved in making the films was able to find a way to keep Watson in the films while giving her enough time to go to college and get the education she wanted. She studied at both Oxford University in England and Brown University in Rhode Island. She graduated from Brown University in May 2014 with a degree in English literature.

During her college years, Watson began practicing **yoga** and **meditation**. She even became a yoga teacher!

13

# MAKING TIME

After filming for the Harry Potter movies was complete, Watson went on to star in other films. She was cast in a supporting role for the film adaptation of the book *The Perks of Being a Wallflower*, which was released in September 2012. She also had a supporting role in the 2013 movie *The Bling Ring* and a number of other films in later years.

Watson became very particular when choosing acting jobs after the Harry Potter movies and turned down several opportunities. She relied on connections with directors and advice from agents, managers, friends, and family to help her make decisions about which movies to be a part of. She wanted to leave herself enough time to focus on her education and on her personal beliefs and ambitions. Watson wanted to **devote** her time to addressing worldwide issues such as poverty and gender inequality.

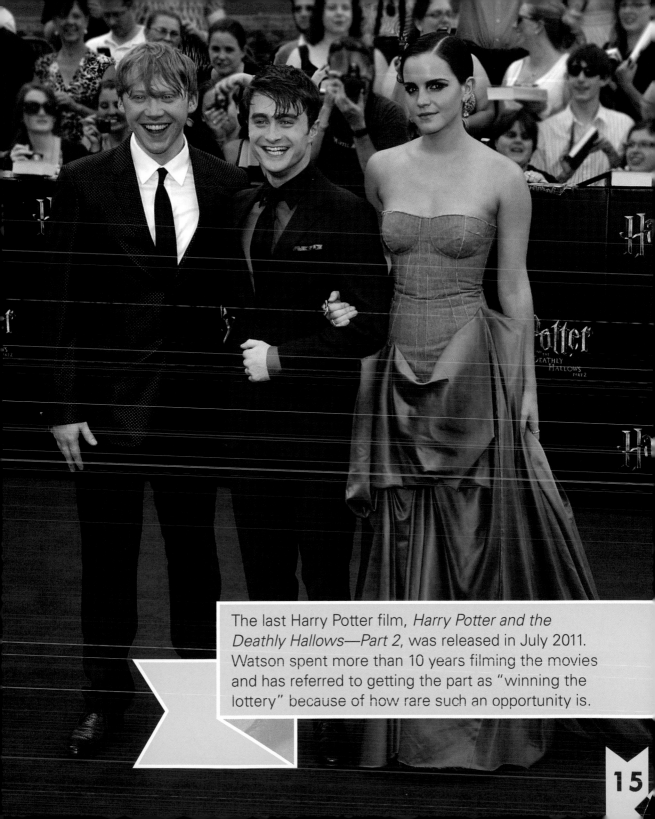

The last Harry Potter film, *Harry Potter and the Deathly Hallows—Part 2*, was released in July 2011. Watson spent more than 10 years filming the movies and has referred to getting the part as "winning the lottery" because of how rare such an opportunity is.

# GIVING BACK

In 2009, Watson joined People Tree, a **fair-trade** clothing company that promotes organic, fashionable clothing made with materials produced in poor and developing countries. The fair trade of materials allows people in those countries to use their skills to produce and sell their goods at a reasonable price, helping create better lives for their families and communities.

In 2012, Watson became an ambassador for Campaign for Female Education (Camfed), an organization **dedicated** to furthering the education of girls in sub-Saharan Africa. The foundation supplies girls with the tools and resources necessary to receive a quality education that would otherwise be unavailable to them. Camfed empowers women in countries where women are treated unequally and works toward creating female leaders in social change

These students attend school in the Kilolo district of Tanzania, Africa. Some female students receive assistance from Camfed to pay for their school and accommodation fees as well as their school uniform costs.

## SEEING THINGS FIRSTHAND

Minimum wage for garment workers in Dhaka, Bangladesh's capital city, is 1,162 taka ($14.42) per week. Companies such as People Tree are working to make a difference. In June 2010, Watson visited People Tree's partner at Swallows in Thanapara, Bangladesh. There, the garment workers are paid a fair wage and are given opportunities to educate themselves and their children. Watson's partnership with People Tree was just the beginning of her efforts to solve worldwide poverty and the issue of **sustainability**.

# AMBASSADOR FOR CHANGE

After Watson graduated from Brown University in 2014, she was appointed a UN Women goodwill ambassador. UN Women is a part of the United Nations that focuses on the empowerment of women and gender equality. This organization helps women become leaders, participate in their countries' political systems as voters and elected officials, and obtain better educational opportunities.

As of 2017, Watson was one of three UN Women goodwill ambassadors. Standing alongside her are actresses Nicole Kidman and Anne Hathaway. It's their job to draw attention to issues relating to women's rights and to promote the ways in which gender inequality can be eliminated. As a feminist and activist for gender equality, this position gives Watson a platform from which to make important changes in

In many parts of the world, women are treated very poorly. UN Women and its goodwill ambassadors work with governments to end violence against all women and girls.

# HeForShe

On September 20, 2014, Watson gave a speech at the United Nations headquarters in New York City. The speech launched a gender equality campaign called HeForShe. The campaign's mission is to get all people to take a stand against gender inequality, arguing that it's an issue that involves and affects not only women, but men too.

Watson's speech described her own personal struggles as a woman and the struggles women everywhere endure on the path to gender equality. She said that gender **stereotypes** aren't just directed toward women. Men also face inequalities and stereotypes, such as being shamed for showing emotion or not acting "manly." Her speech invited everyone—both men and women—to help find a solution to gender inequality.

Watson's speech for the HeForShe campaign had a very powerful message about fighting for gender equality—"If not me, who? If not now, when?"

## HeForShe EFFORTS

In September 2016, Watson gave another speech that highlighted gender inequality in universities. The HeForShe IMPACT 10x10x10 project involves 10 heads of state, 10 global chief executive officers (CEOs), and 10 university presidents from around the world coming together to work toward gender equality in companies, classrooms, and world capitals. The 10 universities reviewed imbalances found in staff positions, course offerings for students, and future career paths.

# OUR
# SHARED SHELF

Watson continues to invite the world to help fight for change. In January 2016, she began an online book club that allows people worldwide to participate in discussions about gender equality. The club is called Our Shared Shelf.

Every month, a new book is chosen, read, and discussed by the group on the Goodreads.com website. Each book relates to feminism and ways people can educate themselves about the gender equality movement. The group has over 192,000 members and gives each person the opportunity to contribute to an open discussion about feminism with other feminists around the world.

It's Watson's hope that the author of each month's book or another knowledgeable person on the book's subject will be able to weigh in on the group's discussion

Watson's interest in feminism goes beyond the written word. She attended the Women's March on Washington on January 21, 2017, to stand up for women's rights in the United States.

## BOOK NINJAS

Watson promotes feminism—and Our Shared Shelf—by hiding books from the club for people to find and read. In March 2017, Watson had people help her hide feminist books in cities worldwide as part of International Women's Day. Each book had a special handwritten note from Watson inside. Earlier in the day, Watson hid books in New York City. In the evening, she helped light the Empire State Building in HeForShe magenta.

# TALE AS OLD

# AS TIME

Even though Watson spends much of her time committed to fighting for gender equality, she still finds time to pursue her acting career. In March 2017, a new version of Disney's *Beauty and the Beast* was released. Watson was cast in the leading role of Belle. As a fan of the fairy tale, Watson was thrilled to play the part of such an intelligent and fierce woman.

The film has been very successful. Much of why it's been so well received is because of the film's modern **interpretation** of the original film. Watson fought for making Belle's character more independent, **innovative**, and practical than the character presented in the previous film. It was important to her that her feminist ideals be reflected in Belle's character.

In *Beauty and the Beast*, Watson starred alongside actor Dan Stevens, who played the Beast.

## COSTUME CHANGES

When Watson accepted the role of Belle, she worked with the film's costume designer to make Belle's wardrobe more adaptable and practical. Small changes to her backstory and costume helped the character appear more independent. Watson chose not to wear a corset, or a tight, stiff piece of clothing worn by women under other clothing to make their waists appear smaller. This choice reflected Watson's views about female beauty and gender equality. Watson also wanted Belle to be more of an inventor than she was in the original film, so pockets were added to her blue dress to act as a sort of tool belt.

# SUSTAINABLE FASHION

Fashion has always been an interest of Watson's. In addition to teaming up with People Tree, she worked as a model for Burberry—a high-end clothing brand—as the face of their fashion campaigns for two years.

It's no surprise that Watson used her love of fashion to continue to promote change. For the *Beauty and the Beast* press tour, Watson requested that the fashion designers who wanted her to wear their clothing answer a set of questions first. She asked that they provide her with information about how the clothing was made and how it impacted the environment. Watson is very careful about the choices she makes and how they can encourage change for a better world, even when it comes to the clothes she's wearing.

Watson and fashion designer Calvin Klein worked together to make the dress she wore to the Met Gala, a fundraising party for the Metropolitan Museum of Art. The dress, pictured here, was made entirely from recycled plastic bottles.

# FIGHTING FOR WHAT'S RIGHT

Many people often consider celebrities to be role models, whether it's because of the characters they play or the issues they fight to fix. From a young age, Emma Watson has dedicated her time to fighting for gender equality and human rights. Through acting, being a UN Women goodwill ambassador, and being a women's rights activist, Watson continues to look for ways to shed more light on gender issues, sustainable fashion, and self-education. She uses her worldwide fame as a way to make a difference in the world.

Her achievements reach much further than her own personal success. Through literature, conversation, and generosity, she stands with many others in an attempt to make the world a better place.

Emma won the first genderless award at the 2017 MTV Movie & TV Awards for best actor for her role in *Beauty and the Beast*.

# TIMELINE

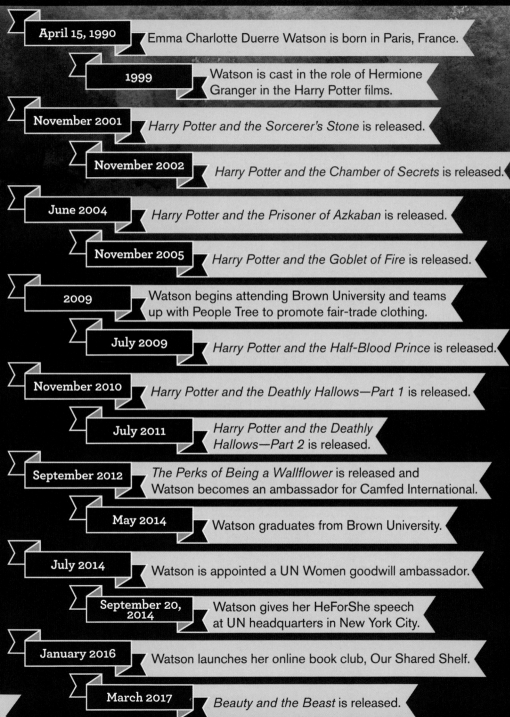

**April 15, 1990** — Emma Charlotte Duerre Watson is born in Paris, France.

**1999** — Watson is cast in the role of Hermione Granger in the Harry Potter films.

**November 2001** — *Harry Potter and the Sorcerer's Stone* is released.

**November 2002** — *Harry Potter and the Chamber of Secrets* is released.

**June 2004** — *Harry Potter and the Prisoner of Azkaban* is released.

**November 2005** — *Harry Potter and the Goblet of Fire* is released.

**2009** — Watson begins attending Brown University and teams up with People Tree to promote fair-trade clothing.

**July 2009** — *Harry Potter and the Half-Blood Prince* is released.

**November 2010** — *Harry Potter and the Deathly Hallows—Part 1* is released.

**July 2011** — *Harry Potter and the Deathly Hallows—Part 2* is released.

**September 2012** — *The Perks of Being a Wallflower* is released and Watson becomes an ambassador for Camfed International.

**May 2014** — Watson graduates from Brown University.

**July 2014** — Watson is appointed a UN Women goodwill ambassador.

**September 20, 2014** — Watson gives her HeForShe speech at UN headquarters in New York City.

**January 2016** — Watson launches her online book club, Our Shared Shelf.

**March 2017** — *Beauty and the Beast* is released.

# GLOSSARY

**activist:** Someone who acts strongly in support of or against an issue.

**adaptation:** Something that is changed so that it can be presented in another form, such as a book, movie, or play.

**audition:** A short performance to test the talents of someone, such as a singer, dancer, or actor.

**dedicate:** To commit to a goal or way of life.

**devote:** To give up to entirely or in part.

**fair trade:** A movement with the goal of helping producers in developing countries get a fair price for their products.

**gender:** The state of being male or female.

**heroine:** A woman admired for great deeds or fine qualities, or the chief female character in a story, poem, or play.

**innovative:** Having or showing new methods or ideas.

**interpretation:** A particular way in which a method or style is changed or applied.

**meditation:** The act or process of spending time in quiet thought.

**stereotype:** A fixed idea that many people have about a thing or a group that may often be untrue or only partly true.

**sustainability:** Able to use methods that don't completely use up or destroy natural resources.

**wizardry:** The magical things done by a wizard, or magician.

**yoga:** A system of exercises for mental and physical health.

# INDEX

# WEBSITES

Due to the changing nature of Internet links, PowerKids Press has developed an online list of websites related to the subject of this book. This site is updated regularly. Please use this link to access the list:
www.powerkidslinks.com/bbios/watson